SMART BLONDE

Willy Holtzman

BROADWAY PLAY PUBLISHING INC
New York
www.broadwayplaypub.com
info@broadwayplaypub.com

Cover art courtesy of City Theatre Company

First edition: January 2023
I S B N: 978-0-88145-844-2

Book design: Marie Donovan
Page make-up: Adobe InDesign
Typeface: Palatino

SMART BLONDE was originally commissioned by City Theatre in Pittsburgh. The play premiered at City Theatre running from 15 November to 21 December 2014. The cast and creative contributors were:

JUDY HOLLIDAY .... Andréa Burns
DAVID OPPENHEIM *(et al)* ....Adam Heller
MAX GORDON *(piano accompaniment, et al)*
.... Jonathan Brody

Director .... Peter Flynn
Set design .... Tony Ferrieri
Costume design .... Robert C T Steele
Lighting design .... Ann Wrightson
Sound design .... Ryan Rumery
Musical supervision & arrangements .... Jonathan Brody
Production stage manager .... Joanna Obuzor

SMART BLONDE opened at 59 E 59 Theaters in Manhattan on 16 March 2019, produced by M B L Productions and Mary J Davis in association with Judith Manocherian L L C. The cast and creative contributors were:

JUDY HOLLIDAY .... Andréa Burns
ELLIOT *and others* .... Mark Lotito
RUTHIE *and others* .... Andrea Bianchi
BERNIE *and others* .... Jonathan Spivey
Understudy .... Garth Kravits
Understudy .... Laura Jordan

Director .... Peter Flynn
Associate director .... Rachel Stevens
Set design .... Tony Ferrieri
Costume design .... Michael McDonald
Lighting design .... Alan Edwards
Sound design .... Joanna Lynne Staub

NOTE ON REFERENCED MUSIC

In addition to the songs on the preceding page
that have been cleared for performance, there is an
additional copyrighted song referenced in this play, for
which permission from the copyright owner(s) must be
obtained for performance, as follows. Other songs may
be substituted provided permission from the copyright
owner(s) of such songs is obtained, or songs in the
public domain may be substituted.

IT MUST BE CHRISTMAS (1961)
by Gerry Mullgan and Judy Holliday
Contact Universal: www.universalmusic.com

(Olmsted Recording Studio—Manhattan)

(1964. Mics on stands, sheet music strewn about, ashtrays brimming with butts. There are empty music stands positioned around the room.)

(BERNIE sits at the piano. ELLIOT, an unseen sound engineer, is in the glass-enclosed control booth.)

ELLIOT: *(On the "God" mic.) What's the Rush? —* instrumental playback, take #1.

(A band track plays over the studio speakers sans vocals.)

(RUTHIE the copyist enters with an armful of sheet music and hands a copy to BERNIE.)

RUTHIE: Here are the new arrangements. *(Listens to the playback)* Not bad.

BERNIE: Maybe a little less bottom on the horns with the remix.

ELLIOT: *(V O)* We'll grab it on the next take when the guys get here.

(The playback stops. BERNIE works out a new tune at the keyboard. RUTHIE checks the musician roster.)

RUTHIE: I see Gerry's got the A Team—Mel, Bobby...

(JUDY HOLLIDAY enters. She is 40 with an incandescent dimpled smile. But the smile is strained. She wears a scarf. She carries a small brown paper bag and a larger shopping bag.)

(BERNIE plays play-on music.)

RUTHIE: And the inimitable vocal stylings of Miss Judy Holliday!

JUDY: *(She curtsies.)* Tyah dah! Who wants coffee? Bernie? Ruthie? *(Places cups on the piano)*

BERNIE: You're the only singer thinks of the musicians.

JUDY: With a voice like mine you *better* think of the musicians. *(Listening to* BERNIE *playing.)* I like that, what is it?

BERNIE: It's brand new. Gerry sent me the chord changes this morning.

RUTHIE: Here's the lead sheet. He said you had the lyrics.

JUDY: I will have finished them by the time he gets here. That's the future perfect tense. Emphasis on TENSE.

BERNIE: Get off it. I've been in the studio with you plenty of times. You're the life of the party.

JUDY: When Gerry's recording. Today it's me. And, I could be wrong, but isn't it hard to sing when you're hyperventilating?

RUTHIE: Hasn't hurt Eartha Kitt. *(Sings, very breathy)* Santa baby.

JUDY: Oh, Elliot—I'm expecting a call.

ELLIOT: *(V O)* I'll patch it through to the studio. Watch for the little red light on the phone.

BERNIE: So I'm looking at the song list. No Comden and Green?

JUDY: What, you don't like Holliday and Mulligan?

BERNIE: I love Holliday and Mulligan! Which brings us to the first song on the list. Elliot?

JUDY: Already?!

BERNIE: To get levels, that's all.

ELLIOT: *(V O) What's The Rush?* —rehearsal take #1.

(The red "Recording" light blinks on in the studio. BERNIE plays the introduction. JUDY steps nervously to the microphone.)

JUDY: What's the rush?
What's the fuss?
Where's the fire?
When you haven't got a thing to do
(She clears her throat, stops singing.) Have we considered back-up singers? Like maybe the Mormon Tabernacle Choir?

BERNIE: You just came in from the cold.

JUDY: *(High, giggly, brassy—Billie Dawn)* You thinkin' you'd like to warm me up, Buster?

RUTHIE: That's it—Billie Dawn's greatest hits! *(As Billie)*
What's the rush?
What's the fuss?

BERNIE: *(Atrociously as Billie)*
Where's the fire?

JUDY: Enough! I'll sing it.

ELLIOT: *(V O)* Still rolling tape.

JUDY: Why do you record rehearsal, Elliot?

ELLIOT: *(V O)* Never know when you might find a keeper. I can mix it down later. Splice in verses, measures, lay it over the band tracks.

JUDY: In other words you can Frankenstein me into a singer? *(A la Dr Frankenstein)* "It's alive!"

ELLIOT: *(V O)* From the top, mastah.

JUDY:
What's the rush?
What's the fuss?

Where's the fire
When you haven't got a thing to do?
(Her voice is diminishing.)

ELLIOT: *(V O)* A little closer to the mic, please.

JUDY: *(Closer)*
Catch a train
Grab a bus
Blow a tire
But you'll never get away from—

JUDY: Hell, I forgot to bring coffee for Elliot.

ELLIOT: *(V O)* I am permanently caffeinated. It's alright, really.

JUDY: It's not alright. There's a Greek deli around the corner.

BERNIE: It's a slight case of nerves. Happens to everyone. We'll work through the song list. It's the best way to get rid of the heebie jeebies! *(Plays Louis Armstrong's* Heebie-Jeebies*)*
Say I've got the heebies
I mean the jeebies
Talkin' about the heebie-jeebies

JUDY: I surrender!

BERNIE: You're thinking about the music too much. Think about something else.

JUDY: Like for instance?

RUTHIE: Like what you did this morning.

JUDY: Now that's fascinating. Let's see, I had my teeth cleaned. I had lunch with my best friend. I had too much wine. Then I did a little Christmas shopping.

BERNIE: What'd you get?

*(*JUDY *proudly removes a baseball mitt from her shopping bag.)*

RUTHIE: How lovely. Bergdorf's or Saks?

JUDY: Modell's! An authentic Rawlings mitt for my son. Gerry told me the brand to get.

BERNIE: How old is Jonathan now?

JUDY: Ten.

BERNIE: Ten already?

JUDY: It all goes too damned fast. Ten is such a fragile age. A kind of last gasp of innocence, you know? I just want to do something really special for him.

RUTHIE: What could be more special for a kid than a baseball mitt?

BERNIE: Except maybe a record album by his mom.

JUDY: Subtle Bernie.

RUTHIE: Is there something you want to talk about, hon?

JUDY: There's nothing to talk about. It's just that this time of year always gets to me. You know, pretty lights, people singing, *cheer*.

RUTHIE: Christmas.

JUDY: Very alienating for a girl from my neighborhood.

RUTHIE: You mean you didn't sit around with Ma and Pa stringing popcorn?

BERNIE: Waiting for Santa to slide down the chimney?

JUDY: In my family we waited for Trotsky. Seriously. And waited. My Uncle Joe used to drag me out in front of his friends and have me recite the names of the original politburo. Lenin, Zinoviev, Kamenev...

BERNIE: I got off easy. I just had to recite the state capitals.

ELLIOT: *(V O)* I'd love to chat with you comrades, but they charge by the hour in this joint.

BERNIE: Now Gerry thought we would come in with an instrumental bridge after the B verse. Elliot?

(The band track instrumental bridge plays for What's The Rush? JUDY *tries to sing over the track.)*

JUDY:
Simmer down
Take it slow
There's a long way to go
How i wish that i could make you see—
(Her voice goes raspy.) Stop recording!

*(*BERNIE *mimes the "cut" signal. The recording light switches off.)*

RUTHIE: Anything I can do?

JUDY: I just need a little time to myself.

BERNIE: Why don't we take five?

*(*JUDY *steps to one side.* BERNIE *and* RUTHIE *retreat to the far side of the piano. We hear the voices in* JUDY's *head.)*

HELEN: Have some tea with lemon.

UNCLE JOE: Sip it through a sugar cube.

BIERLY: This is your F B I dossier. It has a list of your fellow travelers.

YETTA: Don't make promises you can't keep.

SENATOR WATKINS: Do you know a lady by the name of Yetta Cohn, C-O-H-N?

HELEN: I don't know what to do with Judy. She's depressed: all she does is eat.

HARRY COHN: What do you weigh, kid?

HELEN: Judy?

HARRY COHN: Judy?

GERRY: Judy?

ALL THE VOICES: Judy? Judy?

JUDY: Okay!

(The VOICES *stop.)*

JUDY: Baby steps. That's how it's done. Baby steps.

ABE: "21"! Nothin's too good for my girls.

JUDY: She's no "girl", Daddy.

ABE: But you're fifteen and you're dining at "21".

JUDY: While Momma's home giving piano lessons to pay the gas bill.

ABE: Helen is stronger than you think.

JUDY: Daddy, I can't leave her alone. The day after you left I had to pull her head out of the oven!

ABE: She likes to clean.

JUDY: With the pilot light off?

ABE: You are a good daughter, Judy. But you can't carry the world on your shoulders. I'm gonna grab a smoke. You girls talk amongst yourselves.

JUDY: *(As* ABE's CHORUS GIRL*)* I'd sneak you a Manhattan, hon, but you're only a kid. Oh, I'll order one and save ya the cherry. Such a big brain, Abe tells me. Hey, I wouldn't like me if I was you. You wanna know why I take baby steps? Okey dokey. Just between us girls— One, baby steps go with this voice o' mine. Two— Now cross your heart ya don't repeat it, it's what you might call a trade secret—baby steps make you stand out bottom and top, if you get my drift. Like any bigger step would send you fallin' ass over teakettle, which, let's face it, is all the boys want anyway, fallin' ass first into their sheets. Baby steps they don't so much notice your general lack of talent.

CHORUS GIRL: Don't notice your lack of education. Don't notice the baby voice you been puttin' on so long ya don't know your own voice no more.

JUDY/CHORUS GIRL: No baby steps for you.

CHORUS GIRL: Not with that big brain of yours, baby girl.

JUDY/CHORUS GIRL: Big steps!

(The Village Vanguard. The past)

(MAX GORDON enters.)

MAX: Get lost, kid. I don't think this is your kind of place.

JUDY: *(Pauses, then joins the past.)* I came in to get out of the rain.

MAX: How you like the poetry?

POET: "Lacerated grey has bitten into your shapeless humility ...."

JUDY: Nice stuff—what do these guys do for an encore—disembowel themselves? You know, Mr Gordon...

MAX: Max.

JUDY: Max—my friends and I have a comedy revue act.

MAX: Who are these "friends"?

JUDY: Adolph Green, I met him at socialist summer camp. He knows Betty Comden from college, and she has a pianist friend named Lenny. I'm Judy Tuvim.

MAX: Where you kids been working?

JUDY: Last week Adolph booked us at the rally for the Joint Anti-Fascist Refugee Committee. The week before, the fundraiser for the Veterans of the Abraham Lincoln Brigade. We work cheap!

MAX: Okay, I'll give you a shot.

JUDY: You will?! I mean, I'll have to check our schedule. Mind if I ask why you're doing this?

MAX: You're cute, you're smart. And it isn't raining.

JUDY/BETTY/LENNY/ADOLPH:
To get yourself the perfect man
Boy, have we got the perfect plan

LENNY/ADOLPH:
Make your kisses sweet as sugar
Your skin as smooth as butter.

JUDY/BETTY:
In your hair—a blooming flower
Your lashes: start to batter

LENNY/ADOLPH:
Paint your lips as red as cherries

JUDY/BETTY:
And hope he's got a lot of dough

LENNY/ADOLPH:
When he says that you're the berries

JUDY/BETTY/LENNY/ADOLPH:
Then finally you'll know:
You've got yourself a nice, hot guy!

POET: *(Wakes from a drunken stupor.)* "Amateurs! You stink!"

(The group retreats off stage.)

ADOLPH: Okay, next time, Judy sings that song.

JUDY: I'm not singing that song again, Adolph.

ADOLPH: Why not?

LENNY: I've got songs.

JUDY: It's not the song Lenny, it's me. Let Betty sing it.

BETTY: I could sing it.

ADOLPH: Judy has to sing it because it's a funny song.

BETTY: Oh, I'm not funny?

ADOLPH: You're funny in that wisecracking sidekick way.

JUDY: And what way am I funny?

ADOLPH: In the way you're going to be in about one minute.

(*Off* JUDY's *stubborn expression*)

JUDY: Now I'm too anxious to be funny.

LENNY: Betty! Think of something funny.

BETTY: Okay, okay…aardvarks…Shriners.

JUDY: Abe's chorus girl!

BETTY: No offense, Judy, but your father's floozy is far from funny.

JUDY: You haven't heard her talk.

ADOLPH: Look, Judy—I can recite Tennyson by heart; I can whistle the entire Shostakovich Symphony Number Two. But you, you're the cute one.

JUDY: So?

ADOLPH: So go out there and be cute.

LENNY: And one, two, one-two-three-four…

(LENNY *plays up tempo play-on music.* JUDY *throws herself into the song with some razzmatazz dance steps and a comical voice.*)

LENNY & BETTY:	JUDY:
Make your kisses sweet as	sugar!
Your skin as smooth as	butter
in your hair—a blooming	flour!
your lashes: start to	batter!
paint your lips as red as	cherries!
and hope he's got a lot of	dough!
when he says that you're the	berries!
then finally you'll know:	what?
you've got yourself a nice, hot	cherry kruller!
(*Button*)	with coffee!

(Applause. JUDY *takes an exaggerated "diva" bow.* YETTA
COHN *approaches. She's a few years older than* JUDY.*)*

YETTA: I'm Yetta Cohn. My friends and I really enjoyed
the show. Why don't you come have some dinner with
us at that little Italian bistro down the block?

JUDY: Sorry, gotta run.

YETTA: How about Monday?

JUDY: Busy.

YETTA: Tuesday?

JUDY: I really appreciate the invitation. But I live with
my mother. And I've got these aunts and uncles who
don't have any kids. Monday, Uncle Joe has me to
dinner. Tuesday, it's Uncle Harry and Aunt Maude.
Wednesday, it's my mother and grandmother.

YETTA: Are you out of your mind? That's no life for a
young person. Grab your bag—you're having dinner
with *us* now! You have been to a restaurant before?

JUDY: I've been to 21!

(An Italian restaurant)

*(We hear "O Sole Mio" by Giovanni Capurro, Eduardo Di
Capua, and Alfredo Mazzucchi.* YETTA *lights a cigarette.)*

JUDY: I'd like a smoke.

*(*YETTA *offers her pack,* JUDY *plucks a cigarette, lights the
filter end, and coughs.)*

YETTA: *(Takes the cigarette from* JUDY*)* You don't light the
filter.

JUDY: *(False sophistication)* That's how we do it in
Budapest.

YETTA: Relax. I ordered you a glass of Chianti.

JUDY: I'm not really legal age.

YETTA: Have some wine.

JUDY: The thing is, your friends…?

YETTA: Uhuh?

JUDY: They're wearing cop uniforms.

YETTA: That's because they're cops. They won't arrest you.

JUDY: My Uncle Joe says all cops are fascists.

YETTA: Do I look like a fascist to you?

JUDY: No, but…you're a cop, too?

YETTA: And I'm packin'! *(Beat)* I edit the *Police Gazette.* So who is this Uncle Joe?

JUDY: Joe Gollomb. My Mom's brother. He used to write for the *Daily Worker,* but now he's an author.

YETTA: And he sips tea through a sugar cube while holding forth at the Cafe Royale with the other would-be Jewish intellectuals.

JUDY: You've met him?

YETTA: I've met his type. He's using you.

JUDY: I don't know what you mean.

YETTA: Don't you? I just met you, and already I know you live for your family.

JUDY: I certainly do not!

YETTA: Then why do you still live at home?

JUDY: I can't afford a place of my own.

YETTA: Get a roommate.

JUDY: *(Eyeing* YETTA*)* Know where I can find one?

YETTA: You know, I broke off an engagement last year because the guy wanted kids?

JUDY: And you didn't?

YETTA: I'm a grown-up. I like being with other grown-ups.

MAX: Places.

(The Vanguard)

JUDY:
I met him this past summer in July,
The fella who would be my guy.
His name is Hubert but I call him Hugh,
And that's a name I've come to rue...

I told my neighbor, "I'm in love with Hugh."
(Pronounced: you)
I told my grocer, "I'm in love with Hugh."
I told my butcher and the cop
And I watched their jaws both drop
All because I said that "I love Hugh."

Now my neighbor leaves me roses on my doorstep,
My grocer brings my groceries for free
The butcher throws in an extra chop,
I get a whistle from the cop.
And the city just gave me its key

Poor Hubert didn't like the competition.
He left me and he isn't coming back.
I looked at all the guys
Who thought they were my prize
And chose the one who really had the knack.

My butcher's name is John,
And when people gossip on,
I just tell them that they don't know jack.

(A midtown apartment)

(JUDY shows YETTA around.)

JUDY: Whattaya think? Two bedrooms, a living room big enough for a small piano, and a skylight!

YETTA: With a hole as big as my fist. Is that a pigeon?

JUDY: Don't you just love the wild life on the West Side?

YETTA: That pigeon has friends. Judy—I have an apartment.

JUDY: This isn't an apartment. It's an *atelier*. We'll have rehearsals. We'll have parties to all hours. We'll have Bohemian frolics.

YETTA: Will we have relatives? Because given a choice between pigeons and your family….

JUDY: I promise not one relative will set foot in this place.

YETTA: Don't make promises you can't keep.

JUDY: Don't talk down to me like everybody else!

YETTA: So don't be everybody's Sweet Little Judy. Be yourself.

JUDY: Okay. This is myself saying MOVE IN WITH ME!

YETTA: I'll think about it.

(The Cafe Royale)

(UNCLE JOE *sips tea through a sugar cube.)*

UNCLE JOE: How are things working out with your fascist roommate?

JUDY: Everyone's a fascist to you, Uncle Joe. Even F D R.

UNCLE JOE: Especially F D R!

JUDY: Uncle Joe—can we not talk politics for a change? I think I'm going to take a break from the Vanguard.

UNCLE JOE: Good. I'll find you a real job writing for the *Daily Worker*.

JUDY: I've got a job.

UNCLE JOE: Acting is not a job, it's a phase. All you ever wanted was to be a writer.

JUDY: That's what you wanted for me. So, what do you think of the act?

UNCLE JOE: It's cute. It isn't Chekhov. What's that thing you do with your voice?

JUDY: This is my voice.

UNCLE JOE: It's lower now. On stage it's higher.

JUDY: Higher is funnier. I do it for comic effect.

UNCLE JOE: It makes you sound vapid. You graduated first in your high school class to…

JUDY: Second.

UNCLE JOE: Sure, if you want to count that lesbian introvert. What are you reading?

JUDY: *Diary of a Country Priest*. In French.

UNCLE JOE: Garbage! It's time you read *War and Peace*.

JUDY: Why is it always Tolstoy? Dostoevsky?

UNCLE JOE: I was born in Saint Petersburg! Russian writers are the only ones worth reading.

JUDY: I'll read it on the train to California.

UNCLE JOE: What are you talking, "California"?

JUDY: The reason I'm taking a break…agents have been coming to see the act. One sent his card backstage to "the pretty one". I thought he meant Lenny. Well, the long and the short of it is we're all going to Hollywood to make a movie with Don Ameche and Carmen Miranda. It's called *Greenwich Village*. A real stretch.

UNCLE JOE: The only thing worse than an actor is a movie actor. Judy, you were brought up to do better things than Hollywood.

JUDY: I don't remember a lot of career guidance from Abe or Helen.

UNCLE JOE: And who paid the bills? Who saw to your political upbringing?

JUDY: There's more to life than politics.

UNCLE JOE: Life *is* politics.

JUDY: Well you didn't mind when I was performing for anti-fascist organizations.

UNCLE JOE: THAT was politics. THIS is showing off. Oh, what the hell? Go. Get it out of your system. But first, I'm going to give you a little lesson in *realpolitik*. You see that man over there?

JUDY: That vagrant?

UNCLE JOE: That is Maurice Schwartz. He used to be one of the great actors of the Yiddish Theatre. Now he's invisible. I, on the other hand, walked in here today, and the cashier asked me to autograph a copy of my new biography of Albert Schweitzer. Let's be practical here.

JUDY: Fine, I get it.

UNCLE JOE: On the Otis Intelligence Test you scored 172.

JUDY: I will not be held hostage to a test score.

UNCLE JOE: Actors are children. What are you going to be when you grow up?

JUDY: Look at me, Uncle Joe—I am grown up.

(*Kisses* UNCLE JOE, *turns to* MAURICE SCHWARTZ)

JUDY: Mr Schwartz?

MAURICE SCHWARTZ: I am Maurice Schwartz.

JUDY: *(Very sophisticated)* An honor to meet you, sir. I'm Judy. And I'm an actress.

TRAIN CONDUCTOR: All aboard the Twentieth Century Limited to Hollywood.

(Musical transition. The Revuers are on their way to Hollywood.)

(20th Century Fox Publicity Department)

JUDY/BETTY/ADOLPH/COMPANY:
It's all for art's sake, remember this,
What money we make we only make for art's sake
We're doing alright tonight so have a great ball
Tomorrow we'll all be back behind the eight ball

It's all for art's sake, and we are here
We have to have the atmosphere
Whatever the way we act is due to the simple fact
That whatever we do
We only do for art's sake.

PRESS AGENT: Hey, sweetheart, Jack Gold, Fox publicity department.

JUDY: How do ya do?

PRESS AGENT: Here's a list of names. Pick one.

JUDY: I've got a name.

PRESS AGENT: "Judy Tuvim"? Too Jewish.

JUDY: I'm Jewish!

PRESS AGENT: That's what you think.

JUDY: Tuvim is the Jewish word for holiday. How about "Holiday?"

PRESS AGENT: I like it. Do you spell that with one "l" or two?

ASSISTANT DIRECTOR: *(V O)* Places. Rolling.

(A sound stage at Fox)

MALE SINGER:
It's all for art's sake, it really is

ADOLPH:
We suffer a lot, an awful lot, for art's sake

BETTY:
Come in and see the latest in apparel

JUDY:
One gal is wearing nothing but a barrel

ALL:
It's all for art's sake the girls who pose

ADOLPH:
In hardly any clothes

ALL:
We're happy if we impress
The critics with our finesse
But whatever we do we only do for art's sake.

ASSISTANT DIRECTOR: *(V O)* And cut.

(Montage of stills from Greenwich Village as the 20th Century Fox theme plays under. A bedraggled ADOLPH *and* BETTY*)*

(A Los Angeles apartment)

*(*ADOLPH *and* BETTY *join* JUDY.*)*

ADOLPH: Judy—I bought a bottle of champagne to celebrate our imminent stardom.

BETTY: Chateau Ralph.

ADOLPH: It set me back four bucks!

BETTY: Notwithstanding Adolph's unenlightened palate, we were halfway out the door to pick you up for the screening when our agent called and said…

ADOLPH/BETTY: "Don't go."

JUDY: Why wouldn't we go to our own screening?

ADOLPH: We've been cut!

BETTY: Our big number that we spent two days shooting.

ADOLPH: The one where I was hilarious and the two of you were showing a lot of leg—it's gone without a trace. Cut!

BETTY: Adolph is being modest. We weren't merely cut—we were fired! They hire you for your talent, but if they catch you using it…. *(Draws a finger across her throat like a knife.)*

JUDY: To hell with them. We'll go back to New York. To the REAL Greenwich Village.

ADOLPH: Not Judy two "L" Holliday.

BETTY: They tore up *our* contracts, not yours.

JUDY: I'll break it. I'm going back East with you.

ADOLPH: Like hell you are. You're just starting. You're going to be a starlet!

JUDY: I don't even know what that means.

BETTY: Think of it as simple geometry. A star is the vertical axis.

JUDY: And a starlet?

BETTY: Horizontal.

ADOLPH: Judy—you're smarter than all these mugs. Don't let them pull you down to their level.

BETTY: This is your shot. Take it, but don't give up who you are. *(Exits)*

JUDY: Adolph—remember that first night we went on at the Vanguard?

ADOLPH: You got cold feet about your big number.

JUDY: Before that. When you stopped by Ma's apartment to pick me up in your best suit.

ADOLPH: My only suit. The one I couldn't afford to have pressed. You made me take off the pants so you could iron them.

JUDY: And what did I tell you?

ADOLPH: "You have the legs of Nijinsky!"

JUDY: *(Playfully punches him)* I said, "It's all going to happen for you." I still believe it.

ADOLPH: Thanks, my friend. *(Kisses her)* Never take "if" for an answer. *(Exits)*

(DARYL ZANUCK's outer office at Fox)

(The SECRETARY preps JUDY.)

SECRETARY: A piece of advice, honey—Mr Zanuck likes girls with a lot up top.

JUDY: Good—I'll dazzle him with my brain.

SECRETARY: A little lower from the top.

(SECRETARY hands JUDY a pair of foam rubber falsies.)

JUDY: This is humiliating.

SECRETARY: This is Hollywood.

(JUDY reluctantly slips the falsies into her bra. A buzzer sounds.)

SECRETARY: Can't keep the boss waiting.

JUDY: You're not going to make me go in there alone?

SECRETARY: Don't worry—it's not feeding time at the zoo, yet.

(The SECRETARY walks JUDY into…)

(ZANUCK's office)

ZANUCK: Miss Holliday.

JUDY: Mr Zanuck.

ZANUCK: Welcome. Make yourself comfortable. That will be all, Miss Howell.

(The SECRETARY nods and exits. JUDY realizes it was all a set-up.)

JUDY: *(Sitting uncomfortably)* Forgive me if I'm a little nervous.

ZANUCK: Nothing to be nervous about. Here, let me put you at ease.

(ZANUCK massages JUDY's shoulders. She stiffens at his touch.)

JUDY: So, about my contract....

ZANUCK: All business. I like that in a woman. You know, my wife was about your age when we first met. I was writing silent movies. She was acting in them.

JUDY: How fascinating.

ZANUCK: She could have made the transition to talkies, too, but she chose to give me three fine children instead. Sometimes I wonder if she really had what it takes to make it in this business. Do you have what it takes, Miss Holliday?

JUDY: People tell me I have some talent.

ZANUCK: To hell with talent. Do you have ambition? Do you have grit?

JUDY: I can be very gritty. I'll have my agent get in touch with you.

ZANUCK: We can take care of that right now. You don't want to be a day player. You want to be a contract player with character parts, maybe even leads.

JUDY: That's my dream.

ZANUCK: This is the place where dreams come true.

JUDY: I'm really running *(late)*.

ZANUCK: Whatever it is, Miss Holliday, it can wait.

(ZANUCK pushes JUDY back onto the couch.)

JUDY: It's just that I'm due on the set. *(Channeling ABE'S CHORUS GIRL)* And I never miss an entrance.

ZANUCK: You're with Daryl F Zanuck. They'll understand

(ZANUCK *starts to unbutton* JUDY's *blouse.*)

JUDY: Mr Zanuck! All I want is a job.

ZANUCK: *(With one hand paws her breasts)* Me, too. *(With the other hand unzips his zipper.)*

JUDY: I'm not that kind of girl.

ZANUCK: Every girl is that kind of girl.

(ZANUCK *lowers himself on top of* JUDY.)

JUDY: Mr Zanuck! Mr Zanuck! Mr Zanuck! STOP!!!

(JUDY *stands.* ZANUCK *falls off her lap.*)

ZANUCK: I can ruin you in this town! I own you!

JUDY: Actually, you own these… *(She removes the falsies one at a time and places them on the couch with as much dignity as she can muster.)* …not me! Thank you.

(Musical transition: something like "New York, New York")

*(*HELEN's *apartment in New York)*

*(*JUDY *enters. It's early morning.)*

JUDY: What are you doing up, Ma?

HELEN: You never came home last night. We don't keep Hollywood hours here.

JUDY: Can we not talk about Hollywood?

HELEN: Where were you? I was worried sick.

JUDY: We all went to Reuben's for breakfast after the party.

HELEN: They don't have a phone at Reuben's?

JUDY: It was too late to call.

HELEN: I called everyone—Betty, Adolph, Lenny.

JUDY: For God's sake, it was their Broadway opening night!

HELEN: Well, life doesn't stop because of Broadway. What about me?

JUDY: You know this is only temporary? I'm not home to stay.

HELEN: We could look for a bigger apartment.

JUDY: It's not about the size of the apartment. I'm not having this conversation with you. I'm going to bed.

HELEN: At least tell me about the show.

JUDY: (*Reads from* The Times *review.*) "*On the Town* is the freshest and most engaging musical to come this way since the golden days of *Oklahoma.*" They might have had the decency to get one pan.

HELEN: Be happy for your friends.

JUDY: I'm happy. Don't I look happy? I'm happy that I'm permanently out of work and getting fatter by the minute! While Betty and Adolph are taking over Broadway.

(*The phone rings.*)

JUDY: I'm not home!

HELEN: (*Answers, on phone*) Hello? Oh, Max. I'm so glad you called. I don't know what to do with Judy. She's depressed. We can't pay the bills. She doesn't look for work. All she does is eat. What? This isn't the Village Vanguard Max Gordon? Oh, the Broadway producer Max Gordon! I'm afraid Judy isn't....

JUDY: (*Snatches the phone. A throaty, actressy voice*) Hello. This is Judy Holliday. Too early? Not at all. In fact, I'm just back from a Broadway opening. (*To* HELEN) Sit down. (*To phone*) Philadelphia? A meeting with Garson Kanin, and Ruth Gordon? The Warwick Hotel. Yes, I think I can find it.

Gee but it's tough to be broke, kid.
It's not a joke, kid—it's a curse.
My luck is changing—it's gotten
From simply rotten to something worse.
Who knows, someday I will win, too;
I'll begin to reach my prime.
Now that I see what our end is,
All I can spend is just my time.

(*A room at* The Warwick Hotel *in Philadelphia*)

JUDY: A great honor to meet you Mr Kanin, Miss Gordon.

GARSON: Care for a pastrami sandwich? I lost my appetite around the time we lost our leading lady.

RUTHIE: Garson is being wry which is to say ironic, not the stale stuff on either side of that pastrami. We didn't lose our leading lady. She got stage fright. Did you know I played one of the Lost Boys in *Peter Pan*? The *Times* critic said I was "ever so gay".

GARSON: If we might talk a moment about *Born Yesterday*?

JUDY: It's brilliant! Sorry to interrupt.

RUTHIE: Go on. I do it all the time.

JUDY: It's not just hilarious; it's political but not polemical. And I love the way you reveal that the smartest person in the room is ultimately the one you least expect it to be.

(JUDY *exchanges a knowing glance with* RUTHIE.)

GARSON: What are your thoughts on your character, Miss Holliday?

JUDY: I think I've got this straight—Billie Dawn is the inamorata of a junkyard baron who's in Washington to buy political influence. But it's a bit of a twist on Pygmalion and Galatea, isn't it, although more in the

George Bernard Shaw vein. The creation re-creates the creator.

RUTHIE: It takes a very smart lady to play dumb.

GARSON: Did you get a chance to look at the Act I gin scene?

(JUDY *nods and puts down the script.*)

RUTHIE: You might need that, dear.

JUDY: I read the scene on the train ride down.

GARSON: You're saying you're off book?

JUDY: Pretty much.

GARSON: Enter. Pour yourself a scotch and soda. That's good. Sashay.

RUTHIE: Billie was in the chorus of *Anything Goes*.

GARSON: Now cross to the card table.

(JUDY *pats her hair as if to reaffirm Billie's stupidity.* RUTHIE *grins approval.*)

GARSON: Deal, while moving your lips with each card, like a kindergartner counting sugar cookies.

RUTHIE: Good, good.

(Continuous into…)

(The Lyceum Theatre, New York)

(Opening night on Broadway. Billie Dawn plays Gin with Harry Brock.)

HARRY BROCK: You're in the Big League now. I want you should watch your step.

JUDY/BILLIE: All right.

HARRY BROCK: You gotta learn to fit in. If not, I can't have you around, and that's no bull.

JUDY/BILLIE: All right.

HARRY BROCK: You got to be careful what you do. And—what you say. Twenty-eight.

JUDY/BILLIE: Twenty-eight?

HARRY BROCK: Twenty-eight!

JUDY/BILLIE: You could use a little education yourself, if you ask me.

HARRY BROCK: Who asked you?

JUDY/BILLIE: Nobody.

HARRY BROCK: So shut up.

JUDY/BILLIE: Can't I talk?

HARRY BROCK: Play your cards.

JUDY/BILLIE: It's a free country.

HARRY BROCK: That's what *you* think.

(JUDY/BILLIE *hums a bit of* Anything Goes *in a baby-doll chorus girl's voice.*)

HARRY BROCK: Do you mind?!

JUDY/BILLIE: Gin. Tyah dah!

(*Backstage at the Lyceum*)

YETTA: Happy opening night!

(YETTA *presents flowers to* JUDY.)

JUDY: (*A big hug*) Yetta!

YETTA: Look at you—from the West Village to Broadway.

JUDY: Only five stops on the #1 train, by way of L A and Philly. Look, I know I haven't done a good job of keeping up since I got back....

YETTA: You've got a life of your own. Now go be with your friends.

JUDY: You're still my best friend. You're coming to Sardi's with us to wait for the reviews.

(The phone rings. JUDY *answers.)*

JUDY: Hello? Settle down, Ma. Cousin Millie? Where? Midtown South Precinct. For what? We'll grab a cab. Quick question—who the hell is Cousin Millie?

(Midtown South Precinct)

DESK SERGEANT: Your *unusual* cousin was soliciting donations by phone for a "charitable" organization. The organizers skipped town with the proceeds and left her to take the fall. She claims they seemed like such *nice fellas.*

*(*YETTA *pulls the* DESK SERGEANT *aside and flashes her badge.)*

YETTA: Sergeant, my friend here should be having the greatest night of her life. Instead, she's trying to spring her cousin who, let's face it, is dumber than dog shit. Can we wrap this thing up?

DESK SERGEANT: Bail is set at three…

YETTA: Ahem.

DESK SERGEANT: One hundred dollars.

JUDY: *(Paying up)* …forty, sixty, eighty, ninety, ninety-five, ninety-six, ninety six and fifty cents…

DESK SERGEANT: That's close enough.

JUDY: Let's go!

YETTA: *(Glancing at her watch)* Sardi's is closed now.

JUDY: Some opening night party.

YETTA: What's that all-night burger joint we used to go to in the Village?

JUDY: The White Cow. They've got the best cream pie in the world.

DESK SERGEANT: If you ladies are finished, I gotta go to the can.

(JUDY *grabs a newspaper.*)

JUDY: That the morning edition?

YETTA: You plan to read the theatre section?

DESK SERGEANT: Whattaya take me for?

(DESK SERGEANT *gives* YETTA *the theatre section and exits.*)

YETTA: *(Reading her review)* "Tonight at the Broadway opening of *Born Yesterday*, a star was born."

JUDY: *(Reads her glowing review.)*
I can't give you anything but love, baby.
That's the only thing I've plenty of, baby.
Dream a while, scheme a while
You're sure to find
Happiness and, I guess,
All those things you've always pined for

(Olmsted Studio—the present)

(JUDY *finishes the song for* BERNIE.)

JUDY:
Gee I'd like to see you looking swell, baby.
Diamond bracelets Woolworth doesn't sell, baby.
Till that lucky day you know darn well, baby,
I can't give you anything,
I can't give you anything,
I can't give you anything but love.

BERNIE: You are in fine voice!

JUDY: It's easier when it's just the two of us.

(ELLIOT, *V O. Clears his voice*)

JUDY: Three.

(RUTHIE *enters.*)

JUDY: Four! But that's my limit. You heard about the introverted singer?

BERNIE: No.

JUDY: Exactly!

BERNIE: I would call your singing "soulful".

JUDY: Ha! I can sell anything.

RUTHIE: Hard to think of you as a saleslady.

JUDY: Yeah? Okay, after the opening, a newspaper columnist calls and asks what else I'm working on. I tell him what I really should be working on is finding a man. It's almost as hard as finding an apartment. I tell him—print every word. I'm eligible as hell and want to get married.

RUTHIE: Sold.

JUDY: Lenny calls.

BERNIE: Mr Bern-*stein*!

JUDY: (*Imitates* LENNY) He says—For God's sake, Judy, you're working on Broadway, not Filene's Basement. (*Herself*) In order to spare us both any further embarrassment, he offers to fix me up with a musician friend named David Oppenheim. Lenny says he's good-looking, an excellent clarinetist. And Jewish. I tell him, "He sounds too good to be true. Exactly how well do you know this guy?" Lenny says, "I found him for you, Judy. I didn't take him out for a test drive."

(DAVID's *apartment*)

(JUDY *and* DAVID *playing Scrabble.*)

DAVID: Erotic. E-R-O-T-I-C. Erotic.

(JUDY *removes her jacket.*)

DAVID: I've never played strip Scrabble, before.

JUDY: I'm more of a crossword person, myself. 37 points.

DAVID: I've got a confession.

JUDY: We don't need to know *everything* about each other right away.

DAVID: When I was overseas during the war, all the guys had snapshots of their girlfriends. I didn't have a girlfriend, so I clipped a picture of you from a magazine and said, "This is my girl!"

JUDY: *(Relieved)* That's your confession?

DAVID: There is one other little thing. I've seen you in *Born Yesterday* three times and, well—your voice is a full octave lower in person than it is on stage. I kind of fell for the girl with the squeaky voice.

JUDY: Is that going to be a problem, Mr Oppenheim?

DAVID: Not insurmountable.

JUDY: Good. Because it's all me. High, low, and everything in between. Anything else I should know about you?

DAVID: Columbia Records just hired me to produce their classical recordings.

JUDY: That's very impressive.

DAVID: Not half as impressive as what you've done.

JUDY: We both have something to celebrate. *(Lays down Scrabble tiles)* Z-U-K-U-N-F-T. "Zukunft."

DAVID: That's a foreign word.

JUDY: You going to challenge it?

DAVID: Well, it's a first date, and I'm a gentleman.

JUDY: A gentleman who is about to be down to his B V Ds. *Zukunft* means "future".
I told my neighbor, "I'm in love with Hugh."
I told the grocer, "I'm in love with Hugh."
I told my butcher and the cop,
And I watched their jaws both drop,
All because I said that "I love Hugh."

(JUDY *and* DAVID *kiss.*)

(*Wedding reception*)

(JUDY *is a bride.* DAVID *stomps on an imaginary wine glass—the culmination of a Jewish wedding.*)

DAVID/BETTY/JUDY: Mazel tov!

JUDY: Betty, what a relief to be back in the Village!

BETTY: A nice little garden apartment, just like you always wanted.

JUDY: And every weekend parties.

DAVID: You mean *soirees.*

BETTY: With *luminaries.*

JUDY: Are we luminaries, Betty?

BETTY: Ask Adolph—if you can pry him away from Garson.

JUDY: Garson!

GARSON: (*Kisses her on the cheek*) Judy! I'm so happy for you.

JUDY: Thanks.

GARSON: I know it's your wedding, but if you don't mind talking some shop—I met with Harry Cohn about *Born Yesterday.*

JUDY: I need a drink.

GARSON: No, it's great news—Columbia green-lit the picture. George Cukor's going to direct.

JUDY: I don't suppose you and Mr Cohn discussed casting?

GARSON: Naturally he came at me with the usual suspects—Rita Hayworth, Lucille Ball, Barbara Stanwyck.

JUDY: You didn't even bring up my name?

GARSON: Let me finish. When Harry was done blowing smoke up my ass, I said, "What about Judy Holliday?"

JUDY: And he said?

GARSON: "You mean that fat Jewish broad?"

JUDY: I hate Harry Cohn!

GARSON: Calm down. I have another picture called *Adam's Rib*. It's at M G M with Hepburn and Tracy. George is directing that one, too. Ruth and I wrote a juicy supporting role for you. It will be like a back door audition for Harry Cohn. Trust me.

(JUDY *as Doris Attinger, the* Adam's Rib *Testimony Scene. Take 1. On the witness stand being cross-examined. We hear something like* Adam's Rib—Interlude *by Miklós Rózsa)*

(A scene from Adam's Rib)

JUDY/DORIS: So I says, "Listen, mister," I says, "You can't have it both ways you know, so make up your mind and don't try to make some kind of part-timer out of me." So he says, "Bite your tongue, fatso". So I says, "You comin' home for supper?" So he says, "I'll write you a letter." So I says, "You coming home after?" So he says, "I'll put an ad in The New York Times personal Column and let you know." So I says, "Don't get too sassy, Mr Attinger." So he says "And don't you be lookin' at me so cockeyed 'cause I don't want to have to shake your head up to straighten 'em out." So I threw it. The pot. So he left mad.

(Harry Cohn's office at Columbia Pictures)

HARRY COHN: Well, I've worked with some fat asses before....

JUDY: Nice to meet you, too, Mr Cohn. You should know I went a few rounds with Mr Zanuck and never left my feet.

HARRY COHN: That's not how he tells it.

JUDY: What is it about you guys? You think every actress has a price tag tied around her ankle. Well I don't know what you think you heard about me, but I'm not for sale.

HARRY COHN: *(Overlapping)* Relax. Zanuck is a putz. Harry Cohn makes pictures. So listen up—Garson thinks he sandbagged me with that little stunt of his at Metro. But this is Columbia. And Columbia doesn't make pictures with fat girls.

JUDY: Let me tell you something, Mr Harry Cohn. I can lose twenty pounds like that. But you'll still be the same horse's ass you are today!

HARRY COHN: We're gonna get along just fine.

(Blue Prelude—*instrumental transition*)

(JUDY *and* DAVID's *apartment*)

(JUDY *enters.*)

JUDY: The dry cleaning wasn't ready.

DAVID: I'll get it tomorrow. Oh, this came for you by messenger.

(DAVID *hands* JUDY *a manila envelope. She removes a small book from the envelope.*)

JUDY: *Red Channels?*

(*Up on an* F B I AGENT.)

F B I AGENT: Field agent report, F B I New York Office. File Number: 100-98813. Subject is an actress of stage, radio, television and screen, and was recently nominated for an Academy Award. Informants report subject affiliation with Communist Front organizations as well as "friendships" with Party members and Fellow Travelers.

DAVID: *(Paging through)* Page 78. You're between Lillian Hellman and Lena Horne. Pretty fancy company.

JUDY: It's not a dinner party, David. It's a blacklist.

DAVID: Look, we all know people who were in the Party.

JUDY: *Everybody* I know was in the Party, including Helen, Uncle Joe, Yetta and—you don't want to know who else.

DAVID: But you weren't. Were you?

JUDY: My own husband is asking if I was ever a member of the Communist Party?

DAVID: That's not what I'm asking.

JUDY: Well I did support... *(Reads from the book)* The "Stop Censorship Committee," and the "Civil Rights Congress," and the "Moscow Arts Theatre!" As for joining the Party...

DAVID: Judy—

JUDY: I never got around to it. Happy?

DAVID: I'm happy I married you. But your family...

JUDY: What about my family?

DAVID: Your Uncle Joe has been filling your head with propaganda since the day you were born.

JUDY: For your information, Uncle Joe kept the family going when Helen was a total basket case.

DAVID: She's still a basket case. How many times does she call every day? How many times do you call back?

JUDY: That's typical mother-daughter stuff.

DAVID: Is it typical for a mother to make contributions to known Communist Front organizations in her daughter's name?

JUDY: Don't put this on Helen, alright?

DAVID: It's not just your career on the line....

JUDY: We haven't done anything wrong. We're going to come out of this just fine.

DAVID: And if we don't?

JUDY: I can play basement dives again and you can play Klezmer music at bar mitzvahs.

(The office of American Business Consultants)

(KENNETH BIERLY enters.)

BIERLY: Welcome to "American Business Consultants." I'm Kenneth Bierly.

JUDY: What a coincidence—some guy with the same name is also on the author's page of Red Channels.

BIERLY: I'm no longer associated with that organization. I'm now a consultant for Columbia Pictures.

JUDY: How convenient for you.

BIERLY: This is your F B I dossier. It has a comprehensive list of your "friends", or should I say "fellow travelers"?

JUDY: I don't choose my friends according to their politics.

BIERLY: Maybe you should start! Now, number one, when you testify before the Committee it's essential to play dumb like your character from *Born Yesterday.*

JUDY: I beg your pardon!

(Prelap: The Academy Awards. We hear "20th Century Fox Theme" by Alfred Newmann.)

OSCAR TELECAST ANNOUNCER: *(V O)* Welcome back to the 23rd annual Academy Awards ceremony coming to you from the Pantages Theatre in Hollywood.

BIERLY: Number / two, give them whatever they want.

OSCAR TELECAST ANNOUNCER: *(V O)* Two of our best actress nominees are currently appearing on

Broadway. They will be joining us by live remote from La Zambra in midtown Manhattan.

JUDY: I know where this is going, so don't even think of asking me to name names.

OSCAR TELECAST ANNOUNCER: *(V O)* Miss Gloria Swanson and Miss Judy Holliday.

BIERLY: Never mind me. What do you think is going to happen if you win an Oscar? You might as well paint a big bull's-eye on your back. / If you win, you lose.

(Oscar night—La Zambra)

OSCAR TELECAST ANNOUNCER: *(V O)* If the winner is unable to accept, Miss Ethyl Barrymore will accept on her behalf. The nominees for best actress are Bette Davis for *All About Eve*, Anne Baxter *All About Eve*, Eleanor Parker *Caged*, Gloria Swanson *Sunset Boulevard*, and Judy Holliday *Born Yesterday*. And the Oscar goes to…

(We lose the audio feed to static. There's a stunned silence in the room.)

BIERLY: If you win, you lose.

(The live feed is restored a moment later, and we hear laughter from the Pantages.)

ETHEL BARRYMORE: *(V O)* I'm very honored to accept this award on behalf of Judy Holliday, who can't be with us tonight because she is on Broadway in *Born Yesterday*. Congratulations Judy!

(Flashbulbs pop as JUDY accepts her Oscar)

JUDY:
Let me sigh, let me cry
When I'm blue.
Let me go way from this lonely town.

Won't be long 'til my song
Will be through,
Cause I know I'm on my last go-round.

(A gavel pounds.)

(A Senate hearing room)

SENATOR WATKINS: Do you solemnly swear that the testimony you are about to give in the matter pending before the Subcommittee of the Judiciary Committee of the United States Senate will be the truth, the whole truth, and nothing but the truth, so help you God?

JUDY: I do.

ARENS: Please state your name.

JUDY: Judy Tuvim.

ARENS: Have you used that name in addition to your assumed name of Judy Holliday?

JUDY: I was born Judy Tuvim.

SENATOR WATKINS: T-U-V-I-M. What language is Tuvim?

JUDY: Hebrew.

SENATOR WATKINS: You may proceed with the questioning, Counselor.

ARENS: Thank you, Senator Watkins. Miss Holliday, I put it to you as a fact that you were one of the entertainers at an event given by the Joint Anti-Fascist Refugee Committee.

JUDY: I don't remember offhand.

ARENS: Do you have any difficulty with your memory?

SENATOR WATKINS: It seems to me that a person in your profession has to have a trained memory.

JUDY: I didn't know then that I would have to have that kind of memory.

ARENS: Were you aware that the event was sponsored by the Communist Party?

JUDY: I don't know anything that I ever did was sponsored by the Communist Party. What was it for, strikers?

ARENS: I do not want to be in the position of testifying. I want to be in the position of interrogating you. Did you have any friends who were Communists?

JUDY: Never.

ARENS: Are you saying you're unwilling to name names of individuals you know who were members of the Communist Party?

JUDY: I would be answering untruthfully were I to say what I didn't know.

ARENS: Adolph Green and Betty Comden, with whom you were associated, have Communist front records, do they not?

JUDY: No.

SENATOR WATKINS: Are you sure of that?

JUDY: I am as sure as I can be of anybody who isn't me.

(ARENS *looks through* JUDY's *dossier for a name.*)

ARENS: Do you know a lady by the name of Yetta Cohn?

(JUDY *fights the impulse to panic. She composes herself.*)

ARENS: Do you know a lady by the name of Yetta Cohn? C-O-H-N?

JUDY: Why do certain names need to be spelled?

SENATOR WATKINS: Do we have to spell out the dangers of the globalist attempt to subvert our free society?

JUDY: I'm just wondering what it is about Jewish names in particular?

ARENS: Are you impugning the integrity of this committee?

JUDY: Oh, no. I was merely asking….

ARENS: We will ask the questions! Are you aware of Yetta Cohn's marital status?

JUDY: I don't see what that has to do with….

ARENS: Has she ever married?

JUDY: She was engaged but broke it off.

SENATOR WATKINS: Then you do know Yetta Cohn.

ARENS: What was the nature of your relationship with her, Miss Holliday?

SENATOR WATKINS: Miss Holliday?

(JUDY *and* YETTA'*s apartment [the past]*)

YETTA: Will we have relatives? Because given a choice between pigeons and your family…

JUDY: I promise not one relative will set foot in this place.

YETTA: Don't make promises you can't keep.

JUDY: Don't talk down to me like everybody else!

YETTA: So don't be everybody's Sweet Little Judy. Be yourself.

JUDY: Okay. This is myself saying MOVE IN WITH ME!

YETTA: I'll think about it.

(JUDY *impulsively kisses* YETTA *on the cheek. They lean back and look at each other a moment. They lean in and kiss each other passionately.*)

(*The hearing room*)

SENATOR WATKINS: Miss Holliday, counsel has asked you a direct question. Do you wish to be held in contempt?

(JUDY *takes a deep breath—do they know about Yetta? Is this blackmail?*)

ARENS: Do you know a lady by the name of Yetta Cohn?!

(JUDY's *demeanor changes. She makes a gesture of checking her coiffure, she flashes her dimples and transforms herself into Billie Dawn.*)

JUDY: Yetta Cohn? Sure.

ARENS: What has been the nature of your association with her?

JUDY: She's my best friend.

ARENS: So the two of you are extremely close.

JUDY: As friends go, yeah.

SENATOR WATKINS: Did you know she was a member of the Communist Party?

JUDY: We didn't really discuss politics. But there has been in my mind a sort of not happy-go-lucky, but irresponsible attitude about my political associations.

ARENS: You are not saying that because of any fear of coercion?

JUDY: No. I get nervous whenever I get a parking ticket.

ARENS: It was not until you received the Academy Award that you renounced the Communist movement, is that correct?

JUDY: I never thought I was a Communist, probably as stupid as I am, if I thought I was a Communist I would have joined the party.

SENATOR WATKINS: You said here that you just did not understand that some of your associates and friends had Communist sympathies. That you had ignorance of that.

JUDY: It sounds terrible, but that is pretty much it. I have always been for my country. But I have been awakened to a realization that I have been irresponsible and slightly…slightly more than slightly stupid.

ARENS: The witness has still refused to answer counsel's question about the nature of her association with / Yetta Cohn.

SENATOR WATKINS: Miss Holliday, it is not our intention to hurt you. That is why we are taking your testimony in closed session. Still it is our duty to protect the American people against the worldwide Communist conspiracy.

JUDY: I appreciate your intentions, Senator. More than you know.

ARENS: Mr Chairman, if I might resume.

SENATOR WATKINS: I respectfully suggest that the witness be released from subpoena.

ARENS: Mr Chairman…*Mr Chairman!*

SENATOR WATKINS: This proceeding is hereby adjourned. *(He pounds the gavel.)*

(Headline: Daily Mirror— "Holliday Admits She Was Communist Dupe.")

JUDY:
All the love I could steal beg or borrow
Wouldn't heal all this pain in my soul.
What is love but a prelude to sorrow
With a heartbreak ahead for your goal.
Here I go, now you know
Why I'm leaving
Got the blues, what can I lose…good-bye.

(Olmsted Studio—present)

JUDY: *(At the microphone)*
Good-bye.
Good-bye.

BERNIE: You didn't give them one name.

JUDY: But I did, Bernie. I gave them Billie Dawn. They tried to blackmail me, and I played dumb.

BERNIE: They had your dossier. They knew you were smarter than every last one of them. And still they bought the act. So when you get down to it, who's dumb?

JUDY: I don't know. All I know is I left that committee room and instantly got sick to my stomach.

BERNIE: Stress?

JUDY: And a slight case of pregnancy. Then my agent called to say my upcoming guest shot on The Bob Hope Show was cancelled because the sponsor complained. Turned out they leaked my "secret" testimony anyway. Suddenly, I was a grave threat to the users of Pepsodent. I won an Oscar and lost my career.

(JUDY and DAVID's apartment)

(JUDY and DAVID sit collapsed on the sofa, exhausted. A baby cries in the next room. JUDY sighs.)

DAVID: My turn.

(Door buzzer)

JUDY: I'll get it.

(DAVID exits. JUDY opens the door for YETTA who is holding a bottle of wine.)

YETTA: How's parenthood going?

JUDY: I haven't slept in a month, David and I are barely talking to each other, and some "patriot" called to say she hopes my child dies so, peachy.

YETTA: Here—you can drink your sorrows away.

JUDY: *(Inspects the label)* Gee, nice stuff.

YETTA: I've got six more cases.

JUDY: For your brand new restaurant!

YETTA: There isn't going to be a restaurant.

JUDY: Of course there is. I drove out to the Island with you and saw it myself.

YETTA: You saw a building with tables and a kitchen. What you didn't see is a liquor license and apparently you never will, if the State Liquor Commission has its way.

JUDY: What are you talking about? You're a cop.

YETTA: An ex-cop whose name came up in Senate subcommittee testimony.

JUDY: You've been blacklisted?

YETTA: I don't think they call it that in the restaurant business. I think the phrase is "You're Fucked!" Before I even served my first meal. Gotta be a record.

JUDY: I'm radioactive. Look—when they brought up your name, I didn't know if / they knew.

(DAVID returns holding a swaddled baby.)

YETTA: Hi, David.

DAVID: Hello, Yetta.

(The door buzzer)

YETTA: I'll get it. *(Exits to answer the door)*

(JUDY nuzzles the baby.)

JUDY: How's my beautiful little boy?

DAVID: Awake. Permanently.

(YETTA *returns with* HARRY COHN.)

JUDY: Harry—what are you doing here?

HARRY COHN: I wanted to meet the newest Communist on the Upper West Side.

JUDY: Not funny. This is my best friend, Yetta Cohn.

HARRY COHN: No relation.

YETTA: I've got to run.

JUDY: Yetta…

YETTA: We'll talk. *(Exits)*

HARRY COHN: What's his name?

DAVID: Jonathan.

HARRY COHN: Very goyishe. Do you mind if Judy and I conduct some business?

JUDY: I want David to hear whatever you have to say. But first let me say for the record—no more dumb blondes!

HARRY COHN: You're giving me orders?

JUDY: I'm just saying, Harry, I played my last dumb blonde in front of those Senate bastards.

HARRY COHN: Lotta good it did you.

DAVID: Do you know what some people are calling her?

HARRY COHN: What they say about me I wouldn't repeat in mixed company.

JUDY: But what's in a name, right, Harry?

HARRY COHN: Ten grand is what! That's what it cost to buy your name off the Blacklist.

JUDY: I appreciate the gesture, Harry. But if you're talking about typecasting me.

HARRY COHN: I'm talking about casting you, which is more than anybody else in the business is doing. Look, I really don't give a rat's ass about your politics. I can make movies with a Red, a pink, or whatever color you are. But I can't make movies with a fat girl, and your contract says I don't have to. What do you weigh, kid?

DAVID: She just gave birth!

JUDY: It's okay. About a hundred fifty, Harry…in / the one fifties.

HARRY COHN: Don't bullshit me.

JUDY: 167—5 less than my I Q.

HARRY COHN: I've got a new script by Garson; I've got Cukor directing; I've got Peter Lawford co-starring, and some unknown named "Lemmon" of all things; and your character is blonde! We start shooting on May 1st. Will I have a svelte leading lady?

DAVID: That's a little soon, isn't it?

JUDY: 127 pounds on day one, I swear it.

(The baby cries.)

DAVID: Don't stop on my account. *(Exits with the baby.)*

HARRY COHN: Two months—you lose forty pounds or I call Kim Novak.

JUDY: Kim Novak can kiss my ass in Macy's window!

*(*JUDY *magically starts to shed weight.)*

(Columbia sound stage)

(The first day of shooting, and JUDY *is stunningly thin.)*

JUDY: Tyah dah!

JACK LEMMON: An honor to meet you Miss Holliday.

JUDY: Likewise, Mr Lemmon.

LEMMON: Okay, let's try that again. Judy.

JUDY: Jack. I understand you're a Harvard boy.

LEMMON: I understand you do the Sunday crossword in ten minutes. I need to ask you something.

JUDY: Shoot.

LEMMON: Can you explain why every time I finish a take Mr Cukor says,

CUKOR: Less dear boy, less?

JUDY: There's no *acting* on George's set. *(To* CUKOR*)* George, did you know Jack plays the piano?

CUKOR: Good. He'll have something to fall back on when his movie career is over, which could be any minute.

JUDY: That bar scene we're about to shoot—when did you ever see a bar without someone playing a piano?

CUKOR: Fine, if it'll keep him from acting. Places. Action.

*(*JUDY *and* JACK *sit at the piano as Gladys Glover and Pete Sheppard.)*

JUDY: Two more days and then I'm nobody again.

JACK: You're not nobody to me. *(Plays piano)*

*(*JUDY *and* DAVID*'s apartment)*

DAVID: *(Reading a copy of* Modern Screen *magazine.)* "Judy Holliday has been the constant companion of newcomer…"

JUDY: You don't really believe that trash, do you David?

DAVID: I don't know what to believe. It's two months since I saw you.

JUDY: I was in Hollywood. Getting my career back on track.

DAVID: What about my career? You think you didn't drag me onto the blacklist with you?

JUDY: You're practically running Columbia Records.

DAVID: The Classical Division. And right now I don't see much future in being "Mr Judy Holliday," especially if you're seeing Jack Lemmon.

JUDY: I am not having an affair *(with)*.

DAVID: Well I am!

JUDY: *(Beat)* Who is it?

DAVID: Does it matter?

JUDY: I figure if my husband is screwing another woman I should know who in case I run into her at the market. You owe me that.

DAVID: Spare me the sanctimony.

JUDY: Okay—people make mistakes. It's not the end of the world. We can still make it work.

DAVID: It's not working. Me here. You out there.

JUDY: I'll tell Harry I want to shoot the next picture entirely in New York. An Oscar has to count for something.

DAVID: It got you blacklisted.

JUDY: Then I'll do a play. We'll move back to the Village. It will be like old times.

DAVID: Judy—listen to me. This "mistake", as you call it, wasn't a mistake.

JUDY: You love this woman?

DAVID: *(Beat)* I'll come back for my things later.

JUDY: You can't just walk out.

DAVID: It's over Judy.

JUDY: We have a son!

DAVID: He'll still have both of us in his life. Just not together.

JUDY: David—I didn't have an affair with Jack Lemmon. It was with Peter Lawford.

DAVID: Goodbye, Judy.

(Exits)

(JUDY *sings* What'll I Do? *by Irving Berlin.*)

JUDY:
Gone is the romance that was so divine;
'Tis broken and cannot be mended.
You must go your way,
And I must go mine.
But now that our love dreams have ended…

What'll I do
When you are far away
And I am blue;
What'll I do?
What'll I do?
When I am wondering who
Is kissing you;
What'll I do?
What'll I do with just a photograph
To tell my troubles to?

When I'm alone with only dreams of you
That won't come true,
What'll I do?

(Olmsted Studio—present)

(JUDY *is at the microphone.*)

BERNIE: That's a keeper. Still rolling, Elliot?

ELLIOT: *(V O)* Shit!

RUTHIE: Our crackerjack sound engineer—asleep at the switch!

ELLIOT: *(V O)* I'll get the next take.

JUDY: I need a break.

RUTHIE: I don't want to alarm you, honey, but the sidemen arrive in twenty minutes.

JUDY: That means I've got nineteen minutes to finish my Christmas song. *(Starts to write on a pad)* Perfect—my pencil broke.

RUTHIE: I've got another one somewhere.

JUDY: About that call, Elliot?

ELLIOT: *(V O)* Nothing yet. Is there some kind of an emergency?

RUTHIE: Your pencil, Madame.

JUDY: What rhymes with "snow"?

RUTHIE: Almost everything.

(Knocking)

(JUDY's apartment)

(Knocking)

JUDY: I'm not home!

(ADOLPH and BETTY enter.)

ADOLPH: You should have your phone checked—nobody picks up.

JUDY: It's not nobody. It's me who's not picking up. And give me my key back, Adolph!

BETTY: Is this a bad time?

JUDY: I have nothing but time now that I'm single again.

ADOLPH: About that script we sent over….

BETTY: Adolph!

ADOLPH: I assume she's catching up on her reading.

JUDY: I read it. A good-hearted switchboard operator fixes everybody's life except her own. It's sweet.

ADOLPH: But?

JUDY: It's a musical. No way am I singing on Broadway.

BETTY: You sang all the time in the old act.

JUDY: Singing at the Vanguard is like singing in the shower—only smaller. *(Beat)* Do you ever miss it?

ADOLPH: Showers?

BETTY: *(Elbowing* ADOLPH. *To* JUDY*)* We miss working with you. This isn't really about singing, is it?

JUDY: I'm fine.

BETTY: You're not fine.

ADOLPH: You're shut away in your apartment.

JUDY: No, really, I'm fine. I'm going to make the same movie over and over the rest of my life, and die alone with twenty-five cats crawling over me.

ADOLPH: See—she's fine.

JUDY: Apparently Tuvims are not good at marriage. I don't know how the two of you do it.

ADOLPH: For one thing, we're not married.

BETTY: To each other.

JUDY: You're together more than most married people. What's the secret?

ADOLPH: Alone, nothing. Together, a legend—Romulus and Remus!

BETTY: Damon and Pythias!

ADOLPH: Leopold and Loeb!

BETTY: What it comes down to is I'm a realist.

ADOLPH: And I'm a dreamist. Mr Words and…

BETTY: Mrs Words.

JUDY: I keep thinking about how simple life was. How happy we were. What happened?

BETTY: Hollywood happened.

ADOLPH: With a little sprinkling of McCarthyism. Come on, it's ten years since we worked together. Say "yes" —it will be like old times. What are you afraid of?

JUDY: You really want to know?

ADOLPH: How bad could it be? *(To* BETTY*)* We just found her with the twenty-five cats.

JUDY: I'm afraid I'd go back to work, never meet anyone again, and turn into my mother. Needy, lonely.

BETTY: That's an impossibility—because you don't have a Judy to live your life through. You ARE Judy.

ADOLPH: Although Helen does make a hell of a brisket.

JUDY: Let me ask you something. This script... *(Picking up the manuscript) Bells Are Ringing*—why'd you write it? Because if I thought you were conspiring to get me back on stage.

BETTY: Uhuh?

JUDY: I might do something drastic, like say "maybe."

ADOLPH: As you know, I never take "if" for an answer. But I can live with "maybe," for a little while.

BETTY: Sleep on it, honey.

JUDY: I'm not sleeping much, lately.

ADOLPH: Then insomnia on it.

BETTY: You're not alone, Judy. Come back and play with us. *(Kisses* JUDY, *exits)*

ADOLPH: When I was down on my luck, you said it was all going to happen for me. Love is going to happen for you. *(Kisses* JUDY'*s forehead, exits)*

(The opening bars of "Bells are Ringing." Segue into jazzy piano music. A small party is in progress.)

(A party at ADOLPH'*s apartment)*

*(*JUDY *makes small talk with unseen guests.)*

JUDY: Oh, nobody throws a party like Betty and Adolph! Yes, I love being back on stage—thanks for asking. Well, the Tony Award is wonderful, of course, and it makes an excellent paperweight.

*(*GERRY MULLIGAN *approaches, drink in hand.)*

JUDY: *(Under her breath) I've got to get the hell out of here!*

GERRY: *(To* JUDY*)* A, C, B flat, G, F, D, C.

JUDY: Excuse me?

GERRY: That's what you said a second ago.

JUDY: I didn't say that.

GERRY: You said words that correspond to those notes. "I've got to get the hell out of here."

JUDY: I said that out loud?

GERRY: Loud enough. I'm Gerry Mulligan.

JUDY: How do you do?

GERRY: I have the feeling we've met before.

JUDY: Do you attend the theatre?

GERRY: Not willingly.

JUDY: The movies?

GERRY: Now and then.

JUDY: So, you're trying to pick me up without knowing who I am?

GERRY: Isn't that the whole concept behind a pick-up? Not that I'm trying to…well, you are a very attractive woman.

JUDY: Tell me something—are you a musician?

GERRY: Yes, I am.

JUDY: No more musicians.

GERRY: A *jazz* musician. I'm sitting in tonight with my man Cannonball Adderly at Birdland. Come on, it'll be a gas. What's your name?

JUDY: Judy. Let's get the hell out of here.

(Birdland)

(We hear GERRY's *baritone sax with a quintet, something like* You Stepped Out of a Dream. JUDY *applauds as the set finishes.* GERRY *joins her at the bar with two bottles of beer.)*

JUDY: That was fabulous, the way Cannonball was so happy for you.

GERRY: I blew a good solo. Why wouldn't he be happy?

JUDY: In my world happiness is a bit more—shall we say—competitive.

GERRY: What—fame doesn't make you happy?

JUDY: So you finally figured out who I am?

GERRY: I knew all along. I didn't want you to think I was coming on to you because you're a celebrity. I mean, a jazz musician is pretty much invisible. And I'm happy with that. I can't even imagine what it's like being you.

JUDY: Right now being me means I'm onstage six days a week. And when I'm offstage, I'm onstage! Don't get me wrong—an actress is always happy to have the work.

GERRY: But that's "actress" happy. What makes you happy?

JUDY: Hmm. Playing catch with my son. Seeing the first forsythia of spring. Reading the back of the cornflakes box with a dinner date that somehow turns into breakfast. *(Catching herself)* Oh, and words.

GERRY: Any words in particular?

JUDY: Well, I've pretty much had my fill of Russian novels. Crossword puzzles help pass the time. But something about lyrics. I never told this to anyone before, —I always dreamed of writing songs.

GERRY: Then write. A star's salary has to buy some writing time. Step out of your life. Do something different. You know, I always wanted to compose songs with *words*. We should work together. *(He applies a highly expert kiss.)*

JUDY: How do I know you're not using my body to get to my brain?

GERRY: How do I know you're not using *my* brain to get to my sax?

JUDY: Well you make that thing sound pretty splendiferous.

GERRY: That's a million dollar word.

JUDY: I got plenty more.

(Another kiss)

JUDY: Quick question?

GERRY: Uhuh?

JUDY: Would you like to read the cornflakes box with me tomorrow morning?

(JUDY sings the first six lines of I Wanna Be Loved By You by Herbert Stothart, Bert Kalmar and Harry Ruby.)

JUDY:
I wanna be loved by you,
Just you and nobody else but you.
I wanna be loved by you alone.
I wanna be kissed by you,
Just you and nobody else but you.
I wanna be kissed by you alone.

(The phone rings.)

MAX GORDON: *(On phone)* Judy, Max. Village Max.

(Back and forth on the phone.)

JUDY: How you been, Max?

MAX GORDON: Bored as shit. I hear you're spending time with Gerry.

JUDY: You called to discuss my love life?

MAX GORDON: You know me better than that. So I'm opening a supper club on East 55th Street—the Blue Angel. Wait'll you see it—pink leather banquettes. Black marble table tops. Grey velour wallpaper.

JUDY: Sounds like a bordello.

MAX: Yeah, yeah. I still got the Vanguard for atmosphere. But I wanna see what it's like to run an upscale joint—at street level. I know it's a few hundred years since you did a cabaret act, but if you've got songs, a few comedy bits....

JUDY: I don't tell jokes. But I do one or two impressions.

(The Blue Angel nightclub)

JUDY: *(On stage a la Marilyn Monroe:)*
I wanna be loved by you,
Just you and nobody else but you.
I wanna be loved by you alone.

Pooh pooh bee doo!

(JUDY is in her dressing room after the show.)

JUDY: This dressing room is worse than the Vanguard.

(*A knock*)

JUDY: Come in, Max.

(MARILYN MONROE *enters.*)

MARILYN: What a dump! That was my Betty Davis impression. Lousy, right?

JUDY: Miss Monroe!

MARILYN: Well, Judy, I think we can be on a first name basis after the "Marilyn" you did tonight.

JUDY: Holy shit! No one told me you were coming. When I get hold of Max, I'm gonna kill him. I've got to apologize. I'm sure I got you all wrong.

MARILYN: Wrong, how?

JUDY: For one thing, when I try to look sexy, I just look fat.

MARILYN: You think you're fat. Look at this. (*Lifts her blouse*)

JUDY: Well, there's fat, and then there's *fat*.

MARILYN: There is one thing, though. Let me show you how to put on *my* face.

(JUDY *and* MARILYN *both face the mirror.*)

MARILYN: Make the eyebrow a little pointier. The beauty mark a little lower. Puff out your lips.

(JUDY *laughs.*)

MARILYN: Let me in on the gag.

JUDY: It just occurred to me—I'm imitating Marilyn Monroe imitating Marilyn Monroe.

MARILYN: I do it every day.

JUDY: These voices they've given us.

MARILYN: My next movie is with Laurence Olivier.

JUDY: Wow!

MARILYN: As an oversexed showgirl! I hear he already refers to me as "the bitch".

JUDY: Harry Cohn called me a "fat Jewish broad."

JUDY/MARILYN: Assholes!

MARILYN: So what are you doing next?

JUDY: A play in New Haven. About Laurette Taylor.

MARILYN: Oh my God, did you actually see her in *The Glass Menagerie?*

JUDY: Well, this play is definitely not Tennessee Williams.

MARILYN: The important thing is you're playing a real woman. You see, that's the big difference between you and me.

JUDY: What?

MARILYN: You found your voice!

(Exits)

JUDY: *(Sings)*
I couldn't aspire
To anything higher
Than to fill the desire
To make you my own.

I wanna be loved by you,
Just you, and nobody else but you.
I wanna be loved by you alone.

(A dressing room at the Shubert Theatre in New Haven)

(GERRY joins JUDY.)

GERRY: How was the house today?

JUDY: *(Her voice is slightly raspy)* Not bad for New Haven. Close your eyes, Gerry. *(Exits Offstage)* Are your eyes closed?

GERRY: Absolutely.

JUDY: *(Offstage)* Close 'em!

(GERRY closes his eyes. JUDY enters with his baritone sax and plays a passable rendition of "Happy Birthday.")

GERRY: You are amazing. *(Kisses her)*

JUDY: Happy Birthday! Gerry I'm…happy! A little exhausted, but happy.

GERRY: What's going on?

JUDY: Sixteen hundred performances of *Born Yesterday*. Nine hundred of *Bells*. No problems. I finally get the dramatic role of a lifetime, and I sound like Carol Channing.

GERRY: It's just a touch of laryngitis. You'll see your doctor on your day off. Let me run down to the Green Room and get you a cup of tea. *(He's at the door.)*

JUDY: Gerry—promise I won't lose my voice.

GERRY: Promise. *(Exits.)*

(We are in JUDY's *head.)*

JUDY: *(To herself)* I'm sorry—do I seem to be losing my voice?

(A sound collage)

DOCTOR: Your throat is fine, Judy. But there was something else on the X-ray and, well, I want you to have some tests. You'll be in and out in thirty minutes.

JUDY: *(Blowing kisses)* I'm ready for my close-up, doctor.

YETTA: Judy?

JUDY: This is taking longer than thirty minutes.

GERRY: Judy?

JUDY: A lot longer.

BERNIE: Judy?

JUDY: Doctor, why is this taking so long?

GERRY: *(Simultaneously)* It's just a touch of laryngitis. You'll see your doctor on your day off. Let me run down to the Green Room and get you a cup of tea.

DOCTOR: *(Simultaneously)* Your throat is fine, Judy. But there was something else on the X-ray and, well, I want you to have some tests. You'll be in and out in thirty minutes.

YETTA: *(Simultaneously)* So don't be everybody's sweet little Judy, be yourself. So don't be everybody's sweet little Judy, be yourself.

(A hospital room)

(YETTA is at JUDY's bedside.)

YETTA: Judy—are you awake?

(JUDY turns away.)

YETTA: This is so unfair. Honey—it's not your fault. There's nothing to be ashamed of.

JUDY: You don't think so? I'm half a woman!

YETTA: You're alive. And half of you is better than a hundred percent of anyone else.

JUDY: In this business? How can I face people?

YETTA: Bullshit.

JUDY: Bullshit? What's bullshit?

YETTA: This isn't you. So here's what's going to happen. You're going to pick up the phone and call that annoying real estate agent with the June Cleaver hair and tell her you want to rent the country house she's been pestering you about. And tomorrow you and I are going to the Flower District to buy...

JUDY/YETTA: Every forsythia we can find!

YETTA: We'll plant them around the house. And if I hear even one syllable of self-pity out of you…. *(Crosses to the door.)*

JUDY: You won't. And Yetta—I love you, too.

(The Olmsted Recording Studio)

(The red light on the phone in the studio flashes.)

ELLIOT: *(V O)* Judy? You've got a call.

(JUDY snaps back to the present. She collects herself, answers.)

JUDY: Hello? Dr Slater?

JUDY: *(On the phone)* Yes, I'm here. Uhuh. I see. More tests. Just as a "precaution". Of course. Whatever you think—caution is good. Huh? Yes, Rawlings. What kid doesn't want a baseball mitt? Uhuh, ten. Ten years old. It's a great age. Every age is a great age! Thank you, Doctor.

(JUDY hangs up the phone. RUTHIE enters.)

JUDY: Maybe I didn't have my teeth cleaned.

RUTHIE: It's really none of my business.

JUDY: Between us girls, I had this "procedure."

RUTHIE: Oh, Sweetheart, I'm so sorry.

JUDY: No—the prognosis is good. That's what the call was about. But the follow-up treatments have been killing my voice. And since it's pretty much all that's left….

RUTHIE: What are you talking about? You could have a show for the asking.

JUDY: But that's the thing. I never had any trouble getting on a stage, in front of a camera. Now it's all I can do to get out the front door. So I write songs.

(JUDY *picks out the opening notes to* It Must Be Christmas *by Gerry Mulligan and Judy Holliday.)*

(BERNIE *enters with* GERRY.)

BERNIE: Look who I found.

GERRY: Is that our song?

JUDY: I've finally got some lyrics.

GERRY: Great!

JUDY: What—no kiss for your collaborator, Mr Mulligan?

(GERRY *plants a big kiss on* JUDY's *lips.)*

JUDY: Better.

GERRY: So, let's hear it.

(JUDY *sits on the piano bench next to* BERNIE. *He plays the chords to* It Must Be Christmas *as she finds the melody.)*

GERRY: Is that really where you want to go with it?

JUDY: Guess I'm not feeling very cheerful. *(Beat)* Gerry, I know.

GERRY: Know what?

JUDY: "Rawlings." The doctor asked about Jonathan's Rawlings mitt.

GERRY: So?

JUDY: So how would he know about that? I didn't buy the glove until after my appointment.

GERRY: *(To* BERNIE *and* RUTHIE) Uh, Bernie? Ruthie?

(BERNIE *and* RUTHIE *exit.)*

JUDY: Did my doctor call you?

GERRY: Let's talk about this later.

JUDY: I asked you a simple question.

GERRY: *(Beat)* Your doctor called me.

JUDY: Because it's a dirty little secret when a woman has a certain disease that attacks a certain part of her body? A secret my doctor couldn't even tell me? It's back.

GERRY: I wanted you to hear it from me. Judy—let's go home.

JUDY: Don't do that. Don't tell me what to do.

GERRY: I'm sorry, what I should have said....

JUDY: I know.

GERRY: Whatever you want.

JUDY: Give me a minute, would you?

GERRY: Sure.

(GERRY exits into the booth. JUDY looks around the studio— she seems to see all the pieces of her life. She sits at the piano and picks out It Must Be Christmas.*)*

(JUDY removes her wig to reveal what's left of her patchy, wispy hair. GERRY re-enters the studio.)

JUDY: Gerry, tell me something—how much does Cannonball weigh?

GERRY: Huh?

JUDY: How much?

GERRY: I don't know.

JUDY: A lot? A little?

GERRY: Definitely not a little.

JUDY: I mean, with a name like "Cannonball"....

GERRY: He's a big guy.

JUDY: Too big to play alto?

GERRY: What does that have to do with...?

JUDY: There are skinnier musicians. Is anybody saying "Don't play those notes—you don't have the right look."

GERRY: That would be crazy. He has chops.

JUDY: I came to the studio today. I got to the door and had to turn back—to go get coffee, I told myself. Coffee for everybody. But it wasn't that. Not really. I was afraid.

GERRY: But these are your....

JUDY: I know they're my friends.

GERRY: Then there's nothing to be afraid (of).

JUDY: You're not hearing me. Look, when I was a kid we had this bathroom that faced the back of a big luxury apartment building. The window had pebbled glass. A curtain someone had stitched together. But I'd only use the bathroom with the lights out. I was afraid people could see in. See me. It's been that way with every room I ever walked into. I'm the wrong size, too plain, too odd, too smart. So I disguise myself. A little peroxide, a push-up bra, a chorus girl voice— "Tyah dah". Let people see *her*. Let them make their opinions, pass judgment. Because it's not me they're judging. It's someone I invented: a dumb, helpless, gentile clay figure. A golem—a Tuvim golem. But when a surgeon takes his scalpel, it's not clay he's cutting. That's me: unprotected, incomplete, diminished. How could I walk in here today? I was too ashamed.

GERRY: Honey, you have nothing to be ashamed of.

JUDY: Look at me, Gerry. *(Beat)* I wanted to do something where it doesn't matter what I weigh, how I look. Dammit I have chops! So I walked into this room and I finished those lyrics. And tomorrow I want to wake up and read the back of the cornflakes box with you. Then we'll go play ball with Jonathan.

GERRY: And the next day?

JUDY: Who knows? But tonight I want to sing my words.

GERRY: So who's stopping you?

(GERRY *kisses* JUDY. *She starts to tie her scarf over her head. She calls out to the booth.*)

JUDY: Bernie? Ruthie? Come on, I know you're listening.

(BERNIE *and* RUTHIE *enter.*)

RUTHIE: Let me help you with that.

(RUTHIE *arranges the scarf on* JUDY's *head, ties a knot.*)

JUDY: What do you think?

RUTHIE: Very *Three Sisters*.

BERNIE: Ready, Judy?

JUDY: Well, the voice ain't much. But it's mine.

(*Beat*)

GERRY: (*Leans towards the microphone*) What's the Rush? music by Gerry Mulligan, lyrics by Judy Holliday. Take one.

(*The "RECORDING" light flashes on.*)

(JUDY *steps back to the microphone.*)

JUDY:
What's the rush?
What's the fuss?
Where's the fire,
When you haven't got a thing to do?

Catch a train.
Grab a bus.
Blow a tire,
But you'll never get away from you

Simmer down.
Take it slow.
There's a long way to go.
How I wish that I could make you see

(The full band track plays underneath.)

JUDY:
That if you would try a steady diet,
Of simple peace and quiet,
In time you'd find,
You might find time for me.

(The studio lights fade. The "RECORDING" light lingers, then blinks off.)

(Projection of an album cover: Holliday With Mulligan.*)*

(Judy Holliday 1921-1965)

(Fade to black)

(A few bars of Gerry Mulligan's Walk on the Water *plays.)*

END OF PLAY